This Mommy's Heart

To my boys,

The best thing that ever happened to me
was becoming your Mama.

I don't feel that there are even words
to describe what you mean to me,
but this book is my attempt.

You are kind, amazing, heart filled humans
that make the world a better place.

Keep doing that. I love you so very much!

Love, Mamacita

This Mommy's Heart

Cynthia Christensen

Advantage
BOOKS

Illustrated by
Marissa Davis

This Mommy's Heart by Cynthia Christensen
Copyright © 2022 by Cynthia Christensen
All Rights Reserved.
ISBN: 978-1-59755-687-3

Published by: ADVANTAGE BOOKS™
               www.advbookstore.com

First Printing: March 2022
22 23 24 25 26 27   10 9 8 7 6 5 4 3 2 1

This Mommy's heart overflows with joy...

Watching your eyes light up just as bright as a full moon sky.

This Mommy's heart grows
quickly warm...

As you hop into my lap and
turn on your charm.

This Mommy's heart feels peace and calm too...

When you are tucked safely in bed
With Jesus' watchful eyes upon you.

This Mommy's heart feels incredibly alive...

Watching you achieve all that for which you strive.

My heart never knew such lively feelings, until my love for you sent it reeling...

You've brought life to the marrow in my bones, and made ever so jovial our wonderful home.

My Father God has given eternal life...

And you, my dear, have been worth the strife,

Nothing compares to the joy of calling you my own.

And nothing ever could make me disown.

These feelings I have, truly they are intense...

Yet imagine even further, a love so immense
that it surpasses all common sense.

A love never-ending and a love that is true...

That is just what the Creator has for you.

This Mommy's heart has a
hole in your shape...

Like a piece of a puzzle
you cannot escape.

This Mommy's heart always misses a beat...

Whenever in life, you experience defeat.

Though I am fashioned
in the image of God...

It is He and He alone
That will never cause
you to sob.

This Mommy's heart longs for perfection...

And never, ever wants to feel rejection.

Yet I know there will be days you will see...
More of the bad than the good in me.

I pray in advance you will forgive me...

For though I try, there will still be times I will cause you to sigh.

I always strive to get it right...

But sometimes I miss my line of sight.

You are most important to me,
And I do always hear your cries...

Yet there may be days I make
you feel otherwise.

The more time that passes the more I will let you see...

That is because I believe the truth, indeed, does set us free.

I never desire to dishonor or mislead...

Rather I'm here to help meet your every need.

With a love that wraps the moon and back, my hearts desire for your life's path...

Is to know your God and know Him well, for He, my child, will make life swell.

A love that is bigger and more perfect each day...

That is my desire, in every way.

This Mommy's heart is
thankful for this...

That He loved me enough
to send you as a gift.

There is no one like you,
And never will be.

Which is precisely, my dear,

Why it is GOOD to be me!